Can anyone be as gloomy as me?

Poems About Being Sad

By **Nick Toczek**

With illustrations
by **Mike Gordon**

*Hodder
Children's
Books*

Text copyright © Nick Toczek 2000

Editor: Sarah Doughty
Designer: Sarah Massini

Published in 2000 by Hodder Wayland,
an imprint of Hodder Children's Books
This edition published in 2005
Reprinted in 2005 and 2006

British Library Cataloguing in Publication Data
Toczek, Nick
Can anyone be as gloomy as me?:
Poems about being Sad
1. Sadness in children – Juvenile poetry
2. Children's poetry, English
1. Title
821.9'14

ISBN 0 3409 1116 6

Printed in China

Hodder Children's Books
A division of Hodder Headline Limited
338 Euston Road, London NW1 3BH

**Most of the illustrations
in this book were first used
in the title 'I Feel Sad'
by Brian Moses.**

Contents

Moody, mardy moany, mo

When you're sad,
how do you know?
Moody, mardy, moany, mo.

No one to play with.
Nowhere to go.
Moody, mardy, moany, mo.

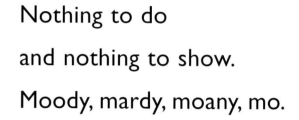

Nothing to do
and nothing to show.
Moody, mardy, moany, mo.

Tick-a-time slowly,
slowly, slow.
Moody, mardy, moany, mo.

It's a cloud you sit below.
Moody, mardy, moany, mo.

The sky inside my head

When sadness gets inside my head
it starts to spread and spread and spread
like buttery jam on a slice of bread,
but it's not yellow and it's not red.

When I told my Grandad this, he said
that it was grey, or blue instead.
So now when I feel sadness spread,
I say the sky has filled my head.

Going to school

RULE 23

Mum! Mum! Don't take me to school!

What if I'm punished for breaking a rule?

What if I fall off a chair or a stool?

What if the teachers are mad, mean and cruel?

What if I'm silly and act like a fool?

What if in swimming I'm pushed in the pool?

Wow! They're playing football, Mum! Isn't school cool!

Can we sit apart, miss?

Please, miss! Christine broke my heart, miss,

tipped her water on my art, miss.

Made me cry, miss, which is why, miss,

like my painting, I'm not dry, miss.

So next time, miss, for a start, miss,

please, please, can we sit apart, miss?

Teacher thinks I'm down in the dumps.

Grandpa winks, says "Cheer up, grumps!"

I get itches, twitches, lumps,
rashes, fever, spots and bumps.

Doc says measles. Mum says mumps.

Gran says: "Chicken-pox, you chumps!"

And I feel poorly.
My head thumps.

Missing Grandma

When Grandma went away by train,
she said: "Now, don't get sad again.
I'm off to see the King of Spain
who carries around a golden cane
to summon the sun and rid him of rain."
But I just wish the King of Spain
would send my Grandma home again.

No good programmes on TV.

And nobody will play with me.

And is it only half-past three?

It's ages till it's time for tea.

So dog and cat and ted agree

they all feel sad for poor old me.

Home from school

All feel sad

When mum and dad are cross and naggy

dog feels sad, his tail's not waggy,

cat feels sad, she's bored and baggy,

plant feels sad, it's leaves are saggy,

day feels sad, gone slow and draggy,

and I'm sad and limp and raggy.

Another thing I'm sad about

Yesterday, my best friend came
home with me. We played a game
of football, until I became
far too rough. I was to blame
when his ball burst. End of game.
He called me a naughty name.
I got cross, called him the same.
So he went home. Now that's a shame.

14

Sulking

Leave me alone. I don't want to play.

I'm sat on my own with nothing to say.

I'm nobody's friend for the rest of today.

So leave me my tea over there on a tray.

And just tell the world that it must go away.

Grounded

Me, my ted, and a dog called Fred...
three sad boys among sad toys
stranded on this bed.

Me, my ted, and a dog called Fred...
grounded here unless we tidy up this mess.
That's what my Mum said.

Saying *sorry*

There was once a little lad.
He'd be moody. He'd be bad.
He'd be rude to Mum and Dad,
shout and scream and get all mad.

When he saw that they were sad
from the tantrum that he'd had,
he would hug them. Then he'd add:
"Sorry!", and they'd all be glad.

It's not fair!

Sadly sitting on a stair.

Sadly with my teddy bear.

Sadly 'cos it isn't fair.

We're up here

    and they're down there.

Now I'm tucked up in my bed.

Prayers and goodnights have been said.

Sadness sneaks out of my head.

Sleep creeps in with gentle tread,

spreads its dreams up there instead,

like curtains made with magic thread.

Sadness goes away

19

How I cheer up

To find the smile

behind my frown,

I *turn* **my** feelings upside *down*.

To lose your frown,

you make it spin:

bottom up, top down,

'til it's a grin.

21

How we cheer up

When we're droopy,
we cheer up,
going loop-de-loopy,
downside up.

Poem to start a new day

Wake up happy. Wake up glad.

Smile at Mum and smile at Dad.

Promise them you won't be sad.

This'll be the best day you've ever had.

Index of first lines

About Nick Toczek

Nick Toczek is too busy to be gloomy.
He's married to Gaynor and they live in
Bradford with two noisy children and an

even noisier cat called
Rover (because they
really wanted a dog).
Nick travels around
Britain working mostly
in schools, libraries
and at festivals.
As well as writing and
performing his poems,
he chats and jokes, makes up and tells
stories, is a wickedly good magician
and uses lots of puppets and masks.
He likes teaching others how to write
and perform.

Photo by Dominic Turner.